Copyright © 2024 by Cyril & Dorise Publishing

All rights reserved.

No part of this publication may be reproduced, distributed, or transmitted in any form or by any means, including photocopying, recording, or other electronic or mechanical methods, without the prior written permission of the publisher, except in the case of brief quotations embodied in critical reviews and certain other non-commercial uses permitted by copyright law.

For permission requests, write to the publisher, addressed "Attention: Permissions Coordinator," at the address below.

Harmony Close,
Kewtown,
Providenciales
Turks & Caicos Islands
ISBN: 9781739369118
https://www.cyrilanddorsiepublishing.com/

Precious Memories... Thoughts Expressed

By
Emily Lorlene Albertha Malcolm
2023

TABLE OF CONTENTS

Dedication 1
Acknowledgement 2
Foreword 3
Introduction 4
Private Thoughts 7
    Life's Mysteries 8
    Holding On? 11
    Hurting 12
    You Have Done The Right Thing 14
    You've Got Me 15
    I Missed You Today 17
    Especially For You 18
    Questions 20
    Why? .... Life Goes On! 21
    If Loving You Means 23
    I Thought About You 24
    We Travelled Together 26
    Control 27
    Looking For Love 29
    I Feel Like 30
    It Is Only You 32
    I Love You 33
    This Is Life 35
    Feelings Expressed 37
    What A Thought! 38

It's Sunrise 40

Emotions 42

My Request 43

Love Is 44

Puzzled 45

Life 46

Thinking About You 47

It Happened Again 48

DEDICATION

I would like to dedicate this book firstly to my loving, adorable parent, Walter and Iris (Tit) Malcolm, who were the epitome of true love. Their expression of love encompassed all with whom they met. They both bore their hearts 'on their sleeves.' I am so proud to have had such wonderful, loving, caring and affectionate parents. I know that I also speak for my siblings, the grandchildren, and great grands when I speak of their genuine love.

I would like to dedicate this book to my siblings and family. Thank you for the unfaltering love and unselfish devotion you have expressed through your actions towards our families and me. You continue to spread and share attributes learnt from our parents.

I would like to dedicate this book to my friends. You never seem to amaze me as you pour your love into others. I will be forever grateful for the pleasure you bring to the lives of so many people because you care and know that 'LOVE' is fundamental in one's relationship with one another.

ACKNOWLEDGEMENT

Firstly, I give honour and thanks to Almighty God, my Lord and Saviour, Jesus Christ for leading and guiding me on my spiritual journey, knowing and understanding the meaning of 'Love', because He first loved me.

I would like to thank my dear friend, Cherry, who in 1999 read and critique most the poems written therein and
gave me the title. Thanks, my friend, for your encouragement and now the realization of a book.

I would also like to acknowledge my friends: Gladys Kennedy and Noreane McKoy and my niece Jade Malcolm, for taking the time to proof the transcript and Ms. Tatianna Hendfield from Cyril Publishing. You are amazing. The quality of my work is as good as it appears because you were all a part of it.

FOREWORD

In "Precious Memories ... Thoughts Expressed", my friend, a long-time educator, has penned these wonderful poems about 'LOVE'.

This book is creatively written about the emotions we all experience associated with 'LOVE', but it is not only 'Love' as the warm fuzzy feelings that we usually conjure up when we think of 'LOVE'.

As we journey through this book we will experience 'LOVE', not only to a degree of great joy and happiness, but pleasure beyond our wildest dream. We will learn that 'LOVE', can also take us to a place of hurt, anger, frustration and pain.

I am sure that you will enjoy and appreciate this anthology of 'LOVE'.

Cherry Whittaker

INTRODUCTION

Many years ago, my Grade 1 student, Zhavago Jolly, then four years old explained that there is a difference between 'Like' and 'Love'. His explanation was that **"Like', is when you talk about your friend, but 'Love' is when you give your friend roses and stuff".** Well, that thought has surely made the realization of this publication possible because of the content therein.

This compilation of poems spans over a period of twenty-five years and so there are those based on 'LIKE' and 'LOVE'. Collectively, they are based on emotions. Emotions are mental states brought on by changes, associated with thoughts, feelings, behavioral responses, and a degree of pleasure or displeasure. It is correct to say that 'Emotions are often intertwined with mood, personality, disposition, or creativity'.

Zhavago, was right about his understanding. Like and Love comprise the following traits:

a. **Friendship which** involves liking someone and sharing a certain degree of intimacy.
b. **Infatuation** often involves intense feelings of attraction without a sense of commitment. It often takes place early in a relationship and may deepen into a more lasting love.
c. **Passionate love** is marked by intense feelings of longing and attraction. It involves an idealization of the other person and a need to maintain constant physical closeness.
d. **Compassionate love** is marked by trust, affection, intimacy, and commitment.
e. **Unrequited love** happens when one person loves another who does not return those feelings.

One must understand that not all forms of love are the same. Psychologists have identified several different types of love that people may experience. Love is marked by being devoted, possessive, and confiding in one another.

According to psychologist Zick Rubin, romantic love is made up of three elements:

- **Attachment**: Needing to be with another person and desiring physical contact and approval
- **Caring**: Valuing the other person's happiness and needs as much as your own
- **Intimacy**: Sharing private thoughts, feelings, and desires with the other person

Whether you are dating, in a relationship, or have been married for years, it is important to learn about the lifelong challenge of maintaining successful romantic relationships. To do so requires deep levels of trust, commitment, and intimacy. Here are some things that one can do to help cultivate loving relationships:

- **Loving-kindness meditation (LKM)-** a technique used to promote self-acceptance and reduce stress, which promotes a variety of positive emotions and improves interpersonal relationships. It involves meditating while thinking about a person you love or care about, concentrating on warm feelings and one's desire for their well-being and happiness.
- **Communication-** everyone's needs are different, so the best way to ensure that one's needs and your loved one's needs are met is to talk about them. Helping another person feel loved involves communicating that love to them through words and deeds. Some ways to do this include showing that you care, making them feel special, telling them they are loved, and doing things for them.
- **Discuss issues in a healthy way** - focus on dealing with issues in ways that move a relationship forward in a positive way.

It is a fact that no relationship is perfect. There will always be problems, conflicts, misunderstandings, and disappointments that can lead to distress or heartbreak. So, while love is associated with a host of positive emotions, it can also be accompanied by several negative feelings as well. Some of the potential pitfalls of experiencing love include anxiety, increased stress, jealousy, depression, sadness, and obsessiveness.

Anyone is bound to experience some negative emotions associated with love. The situation can become problematic if those negative feelings outweigh the positive or if they start to interfere with either person's ability to function normally. Most depressed people do not love themselves and they do not feel loved by others. There is hope for either partner whereby couples needing help to cope with miscommunication, stress, or emotional issues can be helped by 'Relationship Counseling'. Love is the best antidepression, but many of our ideas about it are wrong. The less loved one feels, the more depressed one becomes, for example self-focused, depriving one of opportunities to learn the skills of love. Being loved is critical for one's mind and body. To feel loved and keep love, one must believe in oneself. There are many ways that one can show love for another. Love is important for human beings and whether one likes or does not like another person, scripture admonishes us to in St. John 13: 34: A new commandment I give to you, that you love one another: just as I have loved you, you also are to love one another.

This book expresses my personal thoughts when I felt loved, when I had doubts about love being reciprocated from another or just the situation when my thoughts ran wild, and I wondered about God's creation and how we as human being can and do relate. To those of you who read this book, it is important to understand your partner, family, friends, and all people when expressing love. You can use different methods and see what generates the best results: Words of affirmation, Quality time, Acts of service, Physical touch. Do not be afraid to express love and receive love.

PRIVATE THOUGHTS

LIFE'S MYSTERIES

I'm watching the waves and how beautiful,
They roll, then curl
And unfold into a
Soft, springy, white foam.

It's no wonder-------
God, in creating, human beings,
Made us, as
Beautiful, and powerful as
The waves.

We too must hang loose.
Lighten up!
Let our uniqueness flow.

The cemented wall
Over which some waves came,
But was a block for some,
Should serve as a reminder,
And mentally become,
Our block, too:

To hard times,
Disappointments or stumbling blocks
Which come our way.

The waves cannot be stopped,
So, they beautifully flow
And so we can be,
Triumphantly, loose, and free.

The gleam of light
From the dark cloud
Hanging from the sky
Has brought much excitement,
That has brightened my feelings.

As the sun now shines in my face
Its beams make me squint.
Life has entered my body.
I am rejuvenated!

What a sensational feeling!
What a tremendous view!

My only wish:
That you were here, to share this bliss.

HOLDING ON?

Holding on?
Holding on indefinitely?
Holding on to what?
Is there true love?

That,
That can never be ----
Causes me to plan,
And think:
S-e-l-f-i-s-h-l-y,
M-e-a-n,
W-o-r-l-d-l-y.

Oh My God!
Do,
Let me refrain!
For LOVE does mean to live with pain.

Thanks for the thoughts expressed,
Kindness shown and
Kindness shown.
Holding on is
God's way of the unknown.

HURTING

I'll hurt for
A very long time
And that I know is true,
Because loving you forever
Was all I want to do.

Some day
I will understand,
But now I keep wondering …. Why?
At this time ……..
My feelings
I will not hide.

YOU HAVE DONE THE RIGHT THING

You have done the right thing,
To tell me
What is going on?

You have done the right thing to warn me.
So, it is my choice,
If I want to hold on.

You have done the right thing,
To show me
That painful path
I would have to tread down.

Honesty, one of your outstanding traits
Paralyzes me as I wonder:
Is this a detour,
That I must make?

Right now
I am in pain:
Hurting deep inside,
The realization setting in, is
That true LOVE
Is not on my side.

YOU'VE GOT ME

You're touching me,
And I'm sweating.

You're holding me,
And I'm freezing.

You're squeezing me,
And I'm stiff.

You've got me,
Sitting on a pin.

You've got me,
Cuddling like a baby.

You've got me,
Standing like a queen.

You've got me,
I'm very, happy,
As happy as a lark!

I MISSED YOU TODAY

I missed you today,
My heart is so sad,
But your memories bring me joy,
So, I am glad for those I have.

My thoughts about you
Are happy,
Yet, I feel blue.
Loving you is still, very much,
All I want to do.

Thoughts are dashing,
Here, there, and everywhere -----------
As wild as wild can be.
Swift as lightening
Forceful and penetrating.

They make me wonder,
What is happening to me?
Then I remember
Oh, how I missed you today!

ESPECIALLY FOR YOU

Because you're always in my thoughts,
I, often meditate,
Never forgetting how you make me feel so great.
Gosh! I wish,
Oh, how I wish they would ever stay:

Interesting,

Anxious
Marvelous

Interactive
Never-failing

Loveable,
Overwhelming,
Vivacious,
Ecstatic!

Note the first letter in the words above,
There you will find,
The statement on my mind:
I AM IN LOVE!

QUESTIONS

Is Love ….., Wonderful?
Is Love ….., Kind?

Questions etched in my thoughts; I'll share:
'Does one love
Over and over again after being hurt?
And 'Will true love always remain'?

You make me
Feel so happy,
Yet I'm confused.
The feeling is:
Your love
I will definitely lose.

If that is what is sure to happen
Let's take a break.
I'll take my time,
And ease away
To save myself
Another heart break.

WHY? …. LIFE GOES ON!

How strange to know,
In life we must flow
Be it with great joy or pain,
Be it with heart break or gain.
Be it with a will to live,
Or worries to kill.

Right now, I'm between
That will, to LOVE,
And that PAIN to refrain,
But darling……..,
You are all and everything,
I want to keep me sane.

IF LOVING YOU MEANS

If loving you means,
We're going to be free,
Then loving you means
A whole lot to me.

If loving you means,
My feelings I must stifle,
Then loving you means
I will crumble.

For all the right reasons
I LOVE YOU so much:
It sure pains my heart
To feel as I do right now …. Out of touch.

YET STILL, I LOVE YOU!

I THOUGHT ABOUT YOU

I thought about you,
And how affectionate
You've become.

It's a mark of noted change …..
Maturity, security, and control.

You're not alone,
In all your struggles, there is a light,
At the end of the tunnel.

Keep the faith, plan wisely.
Believe in better days ahead,
Because hard times too will soon end!

Our children are our jewels ---- Precious
Beautifully created by
God's marvelous hands,
So, leave them there,
To be properly cared for.

Pray for strength,
To run your race with endurance
To the end of your day.

Let love abide.
As you always say:
"This too we'll ride,
Christ is the head of our lives".

WE TRAVELLED TOGETHER

I've been with you,
Wherever you went,
Whatever you felt,
And whatever you experienced.
I listened to whatever crossed your mind.

Yes, some painful experiences ….
Almost unrealistic to imagine,
But, factual and true.
Almost everything to make,
One's world blue.

You gave every effort,
Your best shot.
You toed the line,
When others
Would have walked away:
Cause you and your dreams,
Point to brighter, sunny days.

It's no wonder,
You're sad and hurt,
And feel remorse.
Remorse ….
Possibly, your only key in view,
But sweetheart,
Grasp the other key nearby,
Survival too ….

Move away.
Don't look back.
Climb every hill.
Descend every valley,
And climb,
Climb until your dreams come true.

CONTROL

Once again you control my thoughts,
To the extent that
Focus is only you.
Right now,
You are my energy.
You are my strength,
You have my heart, cupped in your hands,
Squeezing love
That has no end.

If I dare say it
Once again,
Reality has struck home:
You are not the man,
I will call my own.

Life circumstances!
Life circumstances!!
Life's circumstances have made this so.
So, whenever you are ready,
Willingly go!

LOOKING FOR LOVE

Have I looked for LOVE,
In all the wrong places?

There was LOVE,
That I should have longed for.
There was LOVE,
That I could have died for.
There was LOVE,
Unlike any other.
There was LOVE,
Without any bother.
There was LOVE,
Without attached strings.
There was LOVE,
To take care of all my needs.

But I looked for LOVE,
In all the wrong places.

Today, I sit and cry,
Because the LOVE I want
Is not at my side.

I often ask myself,
Why?
Would I have been treated differently?
Would I have found LOVE?

Did I allow LOVE to flee?
It was a good thing that I could see.

If not:
LOVE for me
Would not have been,
In the wrong place.

I FEEL LIKE

Mentally disturbed,
Emotionally irritable\
Spiritually empty
Educationally deranged
Because I'm hoping ….,

What I feel
For someone special
Is being felt,
For me
By that someone special too.

I have heard the sentiments,
But are they true?
I feel like
Hope for this affair
Is taking a path,
That
God controls.

I feel like …….

IT IS ONLY YOU

I've thought it through,
A thousand times
And honey,
You're going to be mine.

I cannot live without you ......
I dare not even if I tried.
We were destined to be,
Throughout eternity.

The love we share,
Is as powerful as
The roaring sea:
The way love,
Ought to be.

I know that,
I LOVE YOU
Without a doubt
And that YOU LOVE ME
Just as MUCH.

I LOVE YOU

Life has not always been good.
Life has not always been bad.
So why do I worry and feel so sad?
Because I love you
Shouldn't I feel glad?

Ever, so often I recall happy moments,
Spent with you:

Precious memories that keep me
From being sad
And make me want to keep on being true,
Just because
I love you!

You are special and sentimental,
In your own way.
One day
Together we will say:
Today is our day,
Because we love each other
In a way that's great.

So, honey, we'll keep it this way,
We surely won't miss,
Whatever God has in store for us.
I Love You and
You Love Me
So, together in Love, we trust.

THIS IS LIFE

I'm here,
And I'm existing:
Very much alive!
I can't do,
What I want to,
Nor say,
What I'd want too either ----
But,
This is life.

Every day
We begin life anew.
Yesterday is history.
Today, is here,
And no one knows,
What it holds.

Tomorrow, is future,
And that's a new story ----
But,
This is life.

The past, prepares us,
For what is to come,
Whether it turns out to be:
Good, bad or
In between.

So, make use of what is now.
Forget about yesterday.
Tomorrow may very well
Be different or,
Not at all.
But,
This is life.

To grieve is a terrible thing,

But to do so, "S-I-L-E-N-T-L-Y",
Is even worse.
Send your troubles,
In the wind,
Speak it loudly.
Let it go -----
Never to return.
If not
You'll continue to say:
This is life.

FEELINGS EXPRESSED

I've had it all so far today,
I've thought life through,
In more than one hundred ways,
But, yet still, these feelings
Won't go away.

I'm convinced because,
I know what's right.
My feelings can't take a flight -----
But I'm sorry,
I must do it right.

I'm desperately lonely.
Maybe this I should not tell ------------
But God knows,
What's in my heart as well?

I often wish that,
I was brave enough,
To let my feelings flow
Cause then,
You'll really know,
What you mean to me!

WHAT A THOUGHT!

If life could only be
What I wanted it to,
Would I be truly happy?

If I could go
Where I wanted to,
Would I find the peace of mind I crave?

If I had the things
That I wanted,
Would they mean that much to me?

Thoughts are dashing,
Like a racing car on a track,
Trying to capture the highest mileage ----
And how?

At some time
I'll have to stop,
And that I do in my own time -----
But then,
I must stop!

And such is life,
And my thoughts,
And my questions.

One day, they will all stop!

Life will go on:
Questions, thoughts
Answered or unanswered.

What 'A Thought'!

IT'S SUNRISE

Its sunrise
And I've never
Been more alert than I am right now.
My world
Seems empty and void.
It's as if there's nothing for me,
To look forward too!

Life is drabbed ----
I'm wondering,
What's my purpose?
For being here?
I'm miserable, unhappy, and sad.

Why?
Do I really know?

My thoughts, ….. everywhere -----.

I have every reason
To be proud of myself,
But,
My feelings
Make me feel wasted.

Am I in touch with myself?
Is it that I'm tormented, arrogant or lonely?
But know, I'm not angry.

I guess …… lonely.
There seems to be no one
To whom I can turn.

If everyone is occupied
With troubles and problems
Then I must deal

With my own.

That thought makes me feel better.

I am feeling better.
Far better than when I started.
My heart is still heavy,
But I am alive.
And I thank God,
I am!

EMOTIONS

Do I have to face you?
Have I committed a crime?
There is a kind of hurt,
That won't go away?
Why did you come my way?

Were you sorry for me?
Did you have something to prove?
Has it ended?

I LOVE YOU!
I don't like what I'm feeling.
I never wanted to feel
The way I do.

Do not sympathize with me,
Or try to fill a void.
In the process
We can both be destroyed.

Life will run its course,
Regardless of the track,
My greatest desire
Is not to stay where I am,
Or ever look back:
All because ………….
I LOVE YOU!

MY REQUEST

Lord, why have I always been alone,
In my quest for LOVE?
Why was I not
The chosen one?

Why have men taken their shots,
Then each walked away?
Why despite the circumstances
Do I always feel that,
I must always stay?

Is there someone special and
I will be greatly blessed?
My thoughts never seem positive,
And certainly, my relationships
Have not been.

So, Lord, in your mysterious way
Send me a soul-mate
In a hurry,
PLEASE!

LOVE IS ……..

Love is something,
That's not always exciting and fun.
It's painful,
It's bitter,
It's a son-of-a-gun.
If you're strong
Then you'll survive.
But weak?
It will cut your heart,
And make you cry.

Sometimes tears undoubtedly will flow.
While at other times
The heart will pain, and,
That you do not want to know.

Whatever your lot,
The same is true,
To be loved is a wonderful feeling.
LOVE can be true!

PUZZLED

I'm still puzzled as to
Why things are the way they are?
Why pain and agony prevent me,
From being who I want to be?

You've left me fond memories ---
But scars, tears,
Feelings suppressed.
They cannot be expressed.

In the long run
What is there to gain?
All I foresee is,
Pain, pain, pain.

Sometimes I get so
Caught up in my thoughts ------
That wishing hoping and planning,
Is all I wrought.

Then I must stop
And quiz myself:
What's the purpose of doing this?
Won't I get hurt in the process?

LIFE

Life can be difficult,
Yet so pleasant and fair.
What would it really be like,
If we were near?

You make me feel so happy.
You make me feel real good.
If only you could be mine
Then life----
I understand.

There are no questions
As for reasons,
Why are men like you hard to find?

One thing I know for sure:
I will hold on
To what will last,
For time is sure to pass.

THINKING ABOUT YOU

I'm thinking about you and cannot recall ….
The times we held each other,
Or romantically called.

Every time was special!
And so are the lingering feelings.
Remembering them,
Reliving them
Make for cherished memories.

Sometimes I'm ashamed,
Of what I did or
Did not do,
Especially when I am not with you.

I often recall,
What being loved felt like
Knowing you were all mine.
How I long to fulfil the wishes,
Bottled up inside.

Every time I'm in this mood,
My thoughts turn to gloom,
And I must remember,
You are not mine,
Someone else's!

IT HAPPENED AGAIN

It happened again,
I thought you were mine
And again
I am left with a pain in my heart!
Why did I believe,
That you would be mine?

Thank You, Lord.
Thank You, Father God,
That I know,
That I am your child.
You will heal me and make me whole,
I trust You, Lord.
Only You will make straight a path for me.

www.ingramcontent.com/pod-product-compliance
Lightning Source LLC
Chambersburg PA
CBHW042121100526
44587CB00025B/4150